CYBER SECURITY AND CYBER LAWS

DR SURESH KUMAR RUDRAHITHLU

This book is dedicated to: My beloved Parents Late R.S.Yadapadithaya Shishila & Late.Premalatha

Contents

CHAPTER ONE

What is Cyber Security?

Cyber Security Introduction :

Cyber Security Basics: Cyber security is the most concerned matter as cyber threats and attacks are overgrowing. Attackers are now using more sophisticated techniques to target the systems. Individuals, small-scale businesses or large organization, are all being impacted. So, all these firms whether IT or non-IT firms have understood the importance of Cyber Security and focusing on adopting all possible measures to deal with cyber threats.

What is cyber security? "Cyber security is primarily about people, processes, and technologies working together to encompass the full range of threat reduction, vulnerability reduction, deterrence, international engagement, incident response, resiliency, and recovery policies and activities, including computer network operations, information assurance, law enforcement, etc." OR Cyber security is the body of technologies, processes, and practices designed to protect networks, computers, programs and data from attack, damage or unauthorized access.

· The term cyber security refers to techniques and practices designed to protect digital data.

· The data that is stored, transmitted or used on an information system. OR Cyber security is the protection of Internet-connected systems, including hardware, software, and data from cyber attacks. It is made up of two words one is cyber and other is security.

· Cyber is related to the technology which contains systems, network and programs or data.

· Whereas security related to the protection which includes systems security, network security and application and information security. Why is cyber security important? Listed below are the reasons why cyber security is so important in what's become a predominant digital world:

· Cyber attacks can be extremely expensive for businesses to endure.

· In addition to financial damage suffered by the business, a data breach can also inflict untold reputational damage.

· Cyber-attacks these days are becoming progressively destructive. Cybercriminals are using more sophisticated ways to initiate cyber attacks.

· Regulations such as GDPR are forcing organizations into taking better care of the personal data they hold. Because of the above reasons, cyber security has become an important part of the business and the focus now is on developing appropriate response plans that minimize the damage in the event of a cyber attack. But, an organization or an individual can develop a proper response plan only when he has a good grip on cyber security fundamentals. Cyber security Fundamentals – Confidentiality: Confidentiality is about preventing the disclosure of data to unauthorized parties.

It also means trying to keep the identity of authorized parties involved in sharing and holding data private and anonymous. Often confidentiality is compromised by cracking poorly encrypted data, Man-in-the-middle (MITM) attacks, disclosing sensitive data.

Standard measures to establish confidentiality include:

· Data encryption

· Two-factor authentication

· Biometric verification

· Security tokens Integrity Integrity refers to protecting information from being modified by unauthorized parties.

Standard measures to guarantee integrity include:

· Cryptographic checksums

· Using file permissions

· Uninterrupted power supplies

· Data backups Availability is making sure that authorized parties are able to access the information when needed.

Standard measures to guarantee availability include:

· Backing up data to external drives

· Implementing firewalls

· Having backup power supplies

· Data redundancy

Types of Cyber Attacks A cyber-attack is an exploitation of computer systems and networks. It uses malicious code to alter computer code, logic or data and lead to cybercrimes, such as information and identity theft.

Cyber-attacks can be classified into the following categories:

1) Web-based attacks

2) System-based attacks Web-based attacks These are the attacks which occur on a website or web applications.

Some of the important web-based attacks are as follows

1. Injection attacks It is the attack in which some data will be injected into a web application to manipulate the application and fetch the required information. Example- SQL Injection, code Injection, log Injection, XML Injection etc.

2. DNS Spoofing DNS Spoofing is a type of computer security hacking. Whereby a data is introduced into a DNS resolver's cache causing the name server to return an incorrect IP address, diverting traffic to the attackers computer or any other computer. The DNS spoofing attacks can go on for a long period of time without being detected and can cause serious security issues.

3. Session Hijacking It is a security attack on a user session over a protected network. Web applications create cookies to store the state and user sessions. By stealing the cookies, an attacker can have access to all of the user data.

4. Phishing Phishing is a type of attack which attempts to steal sensitive information like user login credentials and credit card number. It occurs when an attacker is masquerading as a trustworthy entity in electronic communication.

5. Brute force It is a type of attack which uses a trial and error method. This attack generates a large number of guesses and validates them to obtain actual data like user password and personal identification number. This attack may be used by criminals to crack encrypted data, or by security, analysts to test an organization's network security.

6. Denial of Service It is an attack which meant to make a server or network resource unavailable to the users. It accomplishes this by flooding the target with traffic or sending it information that triggers a crash. It uses the single system and single internet connection to attack a server. It can be classified into the followingVolume-based

attacks- Its goal is to saturate the bandwidth of the attacked site, and is measured in bit per second. Protocol attacks- It consumes actual server resources, and is measured in a packet. Application layer attacks- Its goal is to crash the web server and is measured in request per second.

7. Dictionary attacks This type of attack stored the list of a commonly used password and validated them to get original password.

8. URL Interpretation It is a type of attack where we can change the certain parts of a URL, and one can make a web server to deliver web pages for which he is not authorized to browse.

9. File Inclusion attacks It is a type of attack that allows an attacker to access unauthorized or essential files which is available on the web server or to execute malicious files on the web server by making use of the include functionality.

10. Man in the middle attacks It is a type of attack that allows an attacker to intercepts the connection between client and server and acts as a bridge between them. Due to this, an attacker will be able to read, insert and modify the data in the intercepted connection. System-based attacks These are the attacks which are intended to compromise a computer or a computer network.

Some of the important system-based attacks are as follows

1. Virus It is a type of malicious software program that spread throughout the computer files without the knowledge of a user. It is a self-replicating malicious computer program that replicates by inserting copies of itself into other computer programs when executed. It can also execute instructions that cause harm to the system

2. Worm It is a type of malware whose primary function is to replicate itself to spread to uninfected computers. It works same as the computer virus. Worms often originate from email attachments that appear to be from trusted senders.

3. Trojan horse It is a malicious program that occurs unexpected changes to computer setting and unusual activity, even when the computer should be idle. It misleads the user of its true intent. It appears to be a normal application but when opened/executed some malicious code will run in the background.

4. Backdoors It is a method that bypasses the normal authentication process. A developer may create a backdoor so that an application or operating system can be accessed for troubleshooting or other purposes.

5. Bots A bot (short for "robot") is an automated process that interacts with other network services. Some bots program run automatically, while others only execute commands when they receive specific input. Common examples of bots program are the crawler, chatroom bots, and malicious bots.

The 7 layers of cyber security should centre on the mission critical assets you are seeking to protect. 1: Mission Critical Assets – This is the data you need to protect

2: Data Security – Data security controls protect the storage and transfer of data.

3: Application Security – Applications security controls protect access to an application, an application's access to your mission critical assets, and the internal security of the application.

4: Endpoint Security – Endpoint security controls protect the connection between devices and the network.

5: Network Security – Network security controls protect an organization's network and prevent unauthorized access of the network.

6: Perimeter Security – Perimeter security controls include both the physical and digital security methodologies that protect the business overall.

7: The Human Layer – Humans are the weakest link in any cyber security posture. Human security controls include phishing simulations and access management controls that protect mission critical assets from a wide variety of human threats, including cyber criminals, malicious insiders, and negligent users. Vulnerability, threat, Harmful acts

As the recent epidemic of data breaches illustrates, no system is immune to attacks. Any company that manages, transmits, stores, or otherwise handles data has to institute and enforce mechanisms to monitor their cyber environment, identify vulnerabilities, and close up security holes as quickly as possible. Before identifying specific dangers to modern data systems, it is crucial to understand the distinction between cyber threats and vulnerabilities.

Cyber threats are security incidents or circumstances with the potential to have a negative outcome for your network or other data management systems. Examples of common types of security threats include phishing attacks that result in the installation of malware that infects your data, failure of a staff member to follow data protection protocols that cause a data breach, or even a tornado that takes down your company's data headquarters, disrupting access. Vulnerabilities are the gaps or weaknesses in a system that make threats possible and tempt threat actors to exploit them.

Types of vulnerabilities in network security include but are not limited to SQL injections, server misconfigurations, cross-site scripting, and transmitting sensitive data in a nonencrypted plain text format. When threat probability is multiplied by the potential loss that may result, cyber security experts, refer to this as a risk.

SECURITY VULNERABILITIES, THREATS AND ATTACKS – Categories of vulnerabilities

· Corrupted (Loss of integrity)

· Leaky (Loss of confidentiality)

· Unavailable or very slow (Loss of availability) – Threats represent potential security harm to an asset when vulnerabilities are exploited - Attacks are threats that have been carried out

· Passive – Make use of information from the system without affecting system resources

· Active – Alter system resources or affect operation

· Insider – Initiated by an entity inside the organization

· Outsider – Initiated from outside the perimeter Computer criminals Computer criminals have access to enormous amounts of hardware, software, and data; they have the potential to cripple much of effective business and government throughout the world. In a sense, the purpose of computer security is to prevent these criminals from doing damage. We say computer crime is any crime involving a computer or aided by the use of one. Although this definition is admittedly broad, it allows us to consider ways to protect ourselves, our businesses, and our communities against those who use computers maliciously. One approach to prevention or moderation is to understand who commits these crimes and why. Many studies have attempted to determine the characteristics of computer criminals. By studying those who have already used computers to commit crimes, we may be able in the future to spot likely criminals and prevent the crimes from occurring.

CIA Triad :

The CIA Triad is actually a security model that has been developed to help people think about various parts of IT security. CIA triad broken down: Confidentiality It's crucial in today's world for people to protect their sensitive, private information from unauthorized access. Protecting confidentiality is dependent on being able to define and enforce certain access levels for information.

In some cases, doing this involves separating information into various collections that are organized by who needs access to the information and how sensitive that information actually is - i.e. the amount of damage suffered if the confidentiality was breached. Some of the most common means used to manage confidentiality include access control lists, volume and file encryption, and Unix file permissions. Integrity Data integrity is what the "I" in CIA Triad stands for.

This is an essential component of the CIA Triad and designed to protect data from deletion or modification from any unauthorized party, and it ensures that when an authorized person makes a change that should not have been made the damage can be reversed. Availability This is the final component of the CIA Triad and refers to the actual availability of your data. Authentication mechanisms, access channels and systems all have to work properly for the information they protect and ensure it's available when it is needed. Understanding the CIA triad The CIA Triad is all about information. While this is considered the core factor of the majority of IT security, it promotes a limited view of the security that ignores other important factors. For example, even though availability may serve to make sure you don't lose access to resources needed to provide information when it is needed, thinking about information security in itself doesn't guarantee that someone else hasn't used your hardware resources without authorization.

It's important to understand what the CIA Triad is, how it is used to plan and also to implement a quality security policy while understanding the various principles behind it. It's also important to understand the limitations it presents. When you are informed, you can utilize the CIA Triad for what it has to offer and avoid the consequences that may come along by not understanding it.

Assets and Threat: What is an Asset?: An asset is any data, device or other component of an organization's systems that is valuable – often because it contains sensitive data or can be used to access such information. For example: An employee's desktop computer, laptop or company phone would be considered an asset, as would applications on those devices. Likewise, critical infrastructure, such as servers and support systems, are assets.

An organization's most common assets are information assets. These are things such as databases and physical files – i.e. the sensitive data that you store

What is a threat: A threat is any incident that could negatively affect an asset – for example, if it's lost, knocked offline or accessed by an unauthorized party. Threats can be categorized as circumstances that compromise the confidentiality, integrity or availability of an asset, and can either be intentional or accidental. Intentional threats include things such as criminal hacking or a malicious insider stealing information, whereas accidental threats generally involve employee error, a technical malfunction or an event that causes physical damage, such as a fire or natural disaster.

Motive of Attackers :The categories of cyber-attackers enable us to better understand the attackers' motivations and the actions they take.

operational cyber security risks arise from three types of actions:

a)inadvertent actions (generally by insiders) that are taken without malicious or harmful intent;

b) deliberate actions (by insiders or outsiders) that are taken intentionally and are meant to do harm; and iii) inaction (generally by insiders), such as a failure to act in a given situation, either because of a lack of appropriate skills, knowledge, guidance, or availability of the correct person to take action Of primary concern here are deliberate actions, of which there are three categories of motivation.

1. Political motivations: examples include destroying, disrupting, or taking control of targets; espionage; and making political statements, protests, or retaliatory actions.

2. Economic motivations: examples include theft of intellectual property or other economically valuable assets (e.g., funds, credit card information); fraud; industrial espionage and sabotage; and blackmail.

3. Socio-cultural motivations: examples include attacks with philosophical, theological, political, and even humanitarian goals. Socio-cultural motivations also include fun, curiosity, and a desire for publicity or ego gratification

Active attacks: An active attack is a network exploit in which a hacker attempts to make changes to data on the target or data en route to the target. Types of Active attacks: Masquerade: in this attack, the intruder pretends to be a particular user of a system to gain access or to gain greater privileges than they are authorized for. A masquerade may be attempted through the use of stolen login IDs and passwords, through finding security gaps in programs or through bypassing the authentication mechanism. Session replay: In this type of attack, a hacker steals an authorized user's log in information by stealing the session ID. The intruder gains access and the ability to do anything the authorized user can do on the website. Message modification: In this attack, an intruder alters packet header addresses to direct a message to a different destination or modify the data on a target machine. In a denial of service (DoS) attack, users are deprived of access to a network or web resource. This is generally accomplished by overwhelming the target with more traffic than it can handle. In a distributed denial-of-service (DDoS) exploit, large numbers of compromised systems (sometimes called a botnet or zombie army) attack a single target.

Passive Attacks: Passive attacks are relatively scarce from a classification perspective, but can be carried out with relative ease, particularly if the traffic is not encrypted. Types of Passive attacks: Eavesdropping (tapping): the attacker simply listens to messages exchanged by two entities. For the attack to be useful, the traffic must not be encrypted. Any unencrypted information, such as a password sent in response to an HTTP request, may be retrieved by the attacker.

Traffic analysis: the attacker looks at the metadata transmitted in traffic in order to deduce information relating to the exchange and the participating entities, e.g. the form of the exchanged traffic (rate, duration, etc.). In the cases where encrypted data are used, traffic analysis can also lead to attacks by cryptanalysis, whereby the attacker may obtain information or succeed in unencrypting the traffic.

Software Attacks: Malicious code (sometimes called malware) is a type of software designed to take over or damage a computer user's operating system, without the user's knowledge or approval.

Hardware Attacks: Common hardware attacks include:

· Manufacturing backdoors, for malware or other penetrative purposes; backdoors aren't limited to software and hardware, but they also affect embedded radiofrequency identification (RFID) chips and memory

· Eavesdropping by gaining access to protected memory without opening other hardware

· Inducing faults, causing the interruption of normal behaviour

· Hardware modification tampering with invasive operations

· Backdoor creation; the presence of hidden methods for bypassing normal computer authentication systems

· Counterfeiting product assets that can produce extraordinary operations and those made to gain malicious access to systems. Cyber Threats-Cyber Warfare:Cyber warfare refers to the use of digital attacks -- like computer viruses and hacking -- by one country to disrupt the vital computer systems of another, with the aim of creating damage, death and destruction.

Future wars will see hackers using computer code to attack an enemy's infrastructure, fighting alongside troops using conventional weapons like guns and missiles. Cyber warfare involves the actions by a nation-state or international organization to attack and attempt to damage another nation's computers or information networks through, for example, computer viruses or denial-of-service attacks.

Cyber Crime: Cybercrime is criminal activity that either targets or uses a computer, a computer network or a networked device.Cyber crime is committed by cybercriminals or hackers who want to make money. Cybercrime is carried out by individuals or organizations. Some cybercriminals are organized, use advanced techniques and are highly technically skilled. Others are novice hackers.

Cyber Terrorism: Cyber terrorism is the convergence of cyberspace and terrorism. It refers to unlawful attacks and threats of attacks against computers, networks and the information stored therein when done to intimidate or coerce a government or its people in furtherance of political or social objectives. Examples are hacking into computer systems, introducing viruses to vulnerable networks, web site defacing, Denial-of-service attacks, or terroristic threats made via electronic communication.

Cyber Espionage: Cyber spying, or cyber espionage, is the act or practice of obtaining secrets and information without the permission and knowledge of the holder of the information from individuals, competitors, rivals, groups, governments and enemies for personal, economic, political or military advantage using methods on the Internet.

Security Policies: Security policies are a formal set of rules which is issued by an organization to ensure that the user who are authorized to access company technology and information assets comply with rules and guidelines related to the security of information. A security policy also considered to be a "living document" which means that the document is never finished, but it is continuously updated as requirements of the technology and employee changes.

We use security policies to manage our network security. Most types of security policies are automatically created during the installation. We can also customize policies to suit our specific environment.

Need of Security policies:

1) It increases efficiency.

2) It upholds discipline and accountability

3) It can make or break a business deal

4) It helps to educate employees on security literacy

There are some important cyber security policies recommendations describe below

Virus and Spyware Protection policy:

· It helps to detect threads in files, to detect applications that exhibits suspicious behaviour.

· Removes, and repairs the side effects of viruses and security risks by using signatures. Firewall Policy:

· It blocks the unauthorized users from accessing the systems and networks that connect to the Internet.

· It detects the attacks by cybercriminals and removes the unwanted sources of network traffic.

Intrusion Prevention policy:

· This policy automatically detects and blocks the network attacks and browser attacks.

· It also protects applications from vulnerabilities and checks the contents of one or more data packages and detects malware which is coming through legal ways.

Application and Device Control:

· This policy protects a system's resources from applications and manages the peripheral devices that can attach to a system.

· The device control policy applies to both Windows and Mac computers whereas application control policy can be applied only to Windows clients.

CHAPTER TWO

Cyber Laws and Cyber Forensics

CYBERSPACE:

Cyberspace can be defined as an intricate environment that involves interactions between people, software, and services. It is maintained by the worldwide distribution of information and communication technology devices and networks. With the benefits carried by the technological advancements, the cyberspace today has become a common pool used by citizens, businesses, critical information infrastructure, military and governments in a fashion that makes it hard to induce clear boundaries among these different groups. The cyberspace is anticipated to become even more complex in the upcoming years, with the increase in networks and devices connected to it.

REGULATIONS:

There are five predominant laws to cover when it comes to cybersecurity: Information Technology Act, 2000 The Indian cyber laws are governed by the Information Technology Act, penned down back in 2000. The principal impetus of this Act is to offer reliable legal inclusiveness to eCommerce, facilitating registration of real-time records with the Government. But with the cyber attackers getting sneakier, topped by the human tendency to misuse technology, a series of amendments followed. The ITA, enacted by the Parliament of India, highlights the grievous punishments and penalties safeguarding the e-governance, e-banking, and e-commerce sectors. Now, the scope of ITA has been enhanced to encompass all the latest communication devices.

The IT Act is the salient one, guiding the entire Indian legislation to govern cybercrimes rigorously:

Section 43 - Applicable to people who damage the computer systems without permission from the owner. The owner can fully claim compensation for the entire damage in such cases.

Section 66 - Applicable in case a person is found to dishonestly or fraudulently committing any act referred to in section 43. The imprisonment term in such instances can mount up to three years or a fine of up to Rs. 5 lakh.

Section 66B - Incorporates the punishments for fraudulently receiving stolen communication devices or computers, which confirms a probable three years imprisonment. This term can also be topped by Rs. 1 lakh fine, depending upon the severity.

Section 66C - This section scrutinizes the identity thefts related to imposter digital signatures, hacking passwords, or other distinctive identification features. If proven guilty, imprisonment of three years might also be backed by Rs.1 lakh fine.

Section 66 D - This section was inserted on-demand, focusing on punishing cheaters doing impersonation using computer resources. Indian Penal Code (IPC) 1980 Identity thefts and associated cyber frauds are embodied in the Indian Penal Code (IPC), 1860 - invoked along with the

Information Technology Act of 2000. The primary relevant section of the IPC covers cyber frauds: Forgery (Section 464) Forgery pre-planned for cheating (Section 468) False documentation (Section 465) Presenting a forged document as genuine (Section 471) Reputation damage (Section 469) Companies Act of 2013 The corporate stakeholders refer to the Companies Act of 2013 as the legal obligation necessary for the refinement of daily operations. The directives of this Act cements all the required techno-legal compliances, putting the less compliant companies in a legal fix. The Companies Act 2013 vested powers in the hands of the SFIO (Serious Frauds Investigation Office) to prosecute Indian companies and their directors. Also, post the notification of the Companies Inspection, Investment, and Inquiry Rules, 2014, SFIOs has become even more proactive and stern in this regard. The legislature ensured that all the regulatory compliances are well-covered, including cyber forensics, e-discovery, and cybersecurity diligence. The Companies (Management and Administration) Rules, 2014 prescribes strict guidelines confirming the cybersecurity obligations and responsibilities upon the company directors and leaders.

NIST Compliance The Cybersecurity Framework (NCFS), authorized by the National Institute of Standards and Technology (NIST), offers a harmonized approach to cybersecurity as the most reliable global certifying body. NIST Cybersecurity Framework encompasses all required guidelines, standards, and best practices to manage the cyber-related risks responsibly.

This framework is prioritized on flexibility and cost-effectiveness. It promotes the resilience and protection of critical infrastructure by: Allowing better interpretation, management, and reduction of cybersecurity risks – to mitigate data loss, data misuse, and the subsequent restoration costs Determining the most important activities and critical operations - to focus on securing them Demonstrates the trust-worthiness of organizations who secure critical assets Helps to prioritize investments to maximize the cybersecurity ROI Addresses regulatory and contractual obligations Supports the wider information security program By combining the NIST CSF framework with ISO/IEC 27001 - cybersecurity risk management becomes simplified. It also makes communication easier throughout the organization and across the supply chains via a common cybersecurity directive laid by NIST.

Final Thoughts As human dependence on technology intensifies, cyber laws in India and across the globe need constant up-gradation and refinements. The pandemic has also pushed much of the workforce into a remote working module increasing the need for app security. Lawmakers have to go the extra mile to stay ahead of the impostors, in order to block them at their advent. Cybercrimes can be controlled but it needs collaborative efforts of the lawmakers, the Internet or Network providers, the intercessors like banks and shopping sites, and, most importantly, the users. Only the prudent efforts of these stakeholders, ensuring their confinement to the law of the cyberland - can bring about online safety and resilience.

ROLE OF INTERNATIONAL LAWS In various countries, areas of the computing and communication industries are regulated by governmental bodies 1 There are specific rules on the uses to which computers and computer networks may be put, in particular there are rules on unauthorized access, data privacy and spamming 1 There are also limits on the use of encryption and of equipment which may be used to defeat copy protection schemes 1

There are laws governing trade on the Internet, taxation, consumer protection, and advertising l There are laws on censorship versus freedom of expression, rules on public access to government information, and individual access to information held on them by private bodies l Some states limit access to the Internet, by law as well as by technical means. INTERNATIONAL LAW FOR CYBER CRIME Cybercrime is "international" that there are ‘no cyber-borders between countries’ l The complexity in types and forms of cybercrime increases the difficulty to fight back è fighting cybercrime calls for international cooperation l Various organizations and governments have already made joint efforts in establishing global standards of legislation and law enforcement both on a regional and on an international scale

THE INDIAN CYBERSPACE Indian cyberspace was born in 1975 with the establishment of National Informatics Centre (NIC) with an aim to provide govt with IT solutions. Three networks (NWs) were set up between 1986 and 1988 to connect various agencies of govt.

These NWs were, INDONET which connected the IBM mainframe installations that made up India’s computer infrastructure, NICNET (the NIC NW) a nationwide very small aperture terminal (VSAT) NW for public sector organisations as well as to connect the central govt with the state govts and district administrations, the third NW setup was ERNET (the Education and Research Network), to serve the academic and research communities. New Internet Policy of 1998 paved the way for services from multiple Internet service providers (ISPs) and gave boost to the Internet user base grow from 1.4 million in 1999 to over 150 million by Dec 2012. Exponential growth rate is attributed to increasing Internet access through mobile phones and tablets. Govt is making a determined push to increase broadband penetration from its present level of about 6%1. The target for broadband is 160 million households by 2016 under the National Broadband Plan.

NATIONAL CYBER SECURITY POLICY National Cyber Security Policy is a policy framework by Department of Electronics and Information Technology. It aims at protecting the public and private infrastructure from cyber attacks. The policy also intends to safeguard "information, such as personal information (of web users), financial and banking information and sovereign data".

This was particularly relevant in the wake of US National Security Agency (NSA) leaks that suggested the US government agencies are spying on Indian users, who have no legal or technical safeguards against it. Ministry of Communications and Information Technology (India) defines Cyberspace as a complex environment consisting of interactions between people, software services supported by worldwide distribution of information and communication technology.

VISION To build a secure and resilient cyberspace for citizens, business, and government and also to protect anyone from intervening in user's privacy.

MISSION To protect information and information infrastructure in cyberspace, build capabilities to prevent and respond to cyber threat, reduce vulnerabilities and minimize damage from cyber incidents through a combination of institutional structures, people, processes, technology, and cooperation.

OBJECTIVE Ministry of Communications and Information Technology (India) define objectives as follows:

· To create a secure cyber ecosystem in the country, generate adequate trust and confidence in IT system and transactions in cyberspace and thereby enhance adoption of IT in all sectors of the economy.

· To create an assurance framework for the design of security policies and promotion and enabling actions for compliance to global security standards and best practices by way of conformity assessment (Product, process, technology & people).

· To strengthen the Regulatory Framework for ensuring a SECURE CYBERSPACE ECOSYSTEM.

· To enhance and create National and Sectoral level 24X7 mechanism for obtaining strategic information regarding threats to ICT infrastructure, creating scenarios for response, resolution and crisis management through effective predictive, preventive, protective response and recovery actions.

INTRODUCTION: CYBER FORENSICS CYBER FORENSICS:

Computer forensics is the application of investigation and analysis techniques to gather and preserve evidence. Forensic examiners typically analyze data from personal computers, laptops, personal digital assistants, cell phones, servers, tapes, and any other type of media. This process can involve anything from breaking encryption, to executing search warrants with a law enforcement team, to recovering and analyzing files from hard drives that will be critical evidence in the most serious civil and criminal cases. The forensic examination of computers, and data storage media, is a complicated and highly specialized process. The results of forensic examinations are compiled and included in reports. In many cases, examiners testify to their findings, where their skills and abilities are put to ultimate scrutiny.

DIGITAL FORENSICS: Digital Forensics is defined as the process of preservation, identification, extraction, and documentation of computer evidence which can be used by the court of law. It is a science of finding evidence from digital media like a computer, mobile phone, server, or network. It provides the forensic team with the best techniques and tools to solve complicated digitalrelated cases. Digital Forensics helps the forensic team to analyzes, inspect, identifies, and preserve the digital evidence residing on various types of electronic devices. Digital forensic science is a branch of forensic science that focuses on the recovery and investigation of material found in digital devices related to cybercrime.

THE NEED FOR COMPUTER FORENSICS Computer forensics is also important because it can save your organization money. ... From a technical standpoint, the main goal of computer forensics is to identify, collect, preserve, and analyze data in a way that preserves the integrity of the evidence collected so it can be used effectively in a legal case.

CYBER FORENSICS AND DIGITAL EVIDENCE: Digital evidence is information stored or transmitted in binary form that may be relied on in court. It can be found on a computer hard drive, a mobile phone, among other places. Digital evidence is commonly associated with electronic crime, or e-crime, such as child pornography or credit card fraud. However, digital evidence is now used to prosecute all types of crimes, not just e-crime. For example, suspects' e-mail or mobile phone files might contain critical evidence regarding their intent, their whereabouts at the time of a crime and their relationship with other suspects. In 2005, for example, a floppy disk led investigators to the BTK serial killer who had eluded police capture since 1974 and claimed the lives of at least 10 victims

n an effort to fight e-crime and to collect relevant digital evidence for all crimes, law enforcement agencies are incorporating the collection and analysis of digital evidence, also known as computer forensics, into their infrastructure. Law enforcement agencies are challenged by the need to train officers to collect digital evidence and keep up with rapidly evolving technologies such as computer operating systems.

FORENSICS ANALYSIS OF EMAIL:

E-mail forensics refers to the study of source and content of e-mail as evidence to identify the actual sender and recipient of a message, data/time of transmission, detailed record of e-mail transaction, intent of the sender, etc. This study involves investigation of metadata, keyword searching, port scanning, etc. for authorship attribution and identification of e-mail scams.

Various approaches that are used for e-mail forensic are:

· Header Analysis – Meta data in the e-mail message in the form of control information i.e. envelope and headers including headers in the message body contain information about the sender and/or the path along which the message has traversed. Some of these may be spoofed to conceal the identity of the sender. A detailed analysis of these headers and their correlation is performed in header analysis.

· Bait Tactics – In bait tactic investigation an e-mail with http: "" tag having image source at some computer monitored by the investigators is send to the sender of e-mail under investigation containing real (genuine) e-mail address. When the e-mail is opened, a log entry containing the IP address of the recipient (sender of the e-mail under investigation) is recorded on the http server hosting the image and thus sender is tracked. However, if the recipient (sender of the e-mail under investigation) is using a proxy server then IP address of the proxy server is recorded. The log on proxy server can be used to track the sender of the e-mail under investigation. If the proxy server's log is unavailable due to some reason, then investigators may send the tactic e-mail containing a) Embedded Java Applet that runs on receiver's computer or b) HTML page with Active X Object. Both aiming to extract IP address of the receiver's computer and e-mail it to the investigators.

· Server Investigation – In this investigation, copies of delivered e-mails and server logs are investigated to identify source of an e-mail message. E-mails purged from the clients (senders or receivers) whose recovery is impossible may be requested from servers (Proxy or ISP) as most of them store a copy of all e-mails after their deliveries. Further, logs maintained by servers can be studied to trace the address of the computer responsible for making the e-mail transaction. However, servers store the copies of e-mail and server logs only for some limited periods and some may not co-operate with the investigators. Further, SMTP servers which store data like credit card number and other data pertaining to owner of a mailbox can be used to identify person behind an e-mail address.

· Network Device Investigation – In this form of e-mail investigation, logs maintained by the network devices such as routers, firewalls and switches are used to investigate the source of an e-mail message. This form of investigation is complex and is used only when the logs of servers (Proxy or ISP) are unavailable due to some reason, e.g. when ISP or proxy does not maintain a log or lack of co-operation by

ISP's or failure to maintain chain of evidence.

· Software Embedded Identifiers – Some information about the creator of e-mail, attached files or documents may be included with the message by the e-mail software used by the sender for composing e-mail. This information may be included in the form of custom headers or in the form of MIME content as a Transport Neutral Encapsulation Format (TNEF). Investigating the e-mail for these details may reveal some vital information about the senders e-mail preferences and options that could help client side evidence gathering. The investigation can reveal PST file names, Windows logon username, MAC address, etc. of the client computer used to send email message.

· Sender Mailer Fingerprints – Identification of software handling e-mail at server can be revealed from the Received header field and identification of software handling e-mail at client can be ascertained by using different set of headers like "XMailer" or equivalent. These headers describe applications and their versions used at the clients to send e-mail. This information about the client computer of the sender can be used to help investigators devise an effective plan and thus prove to be very useful. EMAIL FORENSICS TOOLS Erasing or deleting an email doesn't necessarily mean that it is gone forever. Often emails can be forensically extracted even after deletion. Forensic tracing of e-mail is similar to traditional detective work. It is used for retrieving information from mailbox files.

· MiTec Mail Viewer – This is a viewer for Outlook Express, Windows Mail/Windows Live Mail, Mozilla Thunderbird message databases, and single EML files. It displays a list of contained messages with all needed properties, like an ordinary e-mail client. Messages can be viewed in detailed view, including attachments and an

HTML preview. It has powerful searching and filtering capability and also allows extracting email addresses from all emails in opened folder to list by one click. Selected messages can be saved to eml files with or without their attachments. Attachments can be extracted from selected messages by one command.

· OST and PST Viewer – Nucleus Technologies' OST and PST viewer tools help you view OST and PST files easily without connecting to an MS Exchange server. These tools allow the user to scan OST and PST files and they display the data saved in it including email messages, contacts, calendars, notes, etc., in a proper folder structure.

· e Mail Tracker Pro – e Mail Tracker Pro analyses the headers of an e-mail to detect the IP address of the machine that sent the message so that the sender can be tracked down. It can trace multiple e-mails at the same time and easily keep track of them. The geographical location of an IP address is key information for determining the threat level or validity of an e-mail message.

· Email Tracer – Email Tracer is an Indian effort in cyber forensics by the Resource Centre for Cyber Forensics (RCCF) which is a premier centre for cyber forensics in India. It develops cyber forensic tools based on the requirements of law enforcement agencies.

DIGITAL FORENSICS LIFECYCLE:

Collection: The first step in the forensic process is to identify potential sources of data and acquire data from them.

Examination: After data has been collected, the next phase is to examine the data, which involves assessing and extracting the relevant pieces of information from the collected data. This phase may also involve bypassing or mitigating OS or application features that obscure data and code, such as data compression, encryption, and access control mechanisms.

Analysis: Once the relevant information has been extracted, the analyst should study and analyze the data to draw conclusions from it. The foundation of forensics is using a methodical approach to reach appropriate conclusions based on the available data or determine that no conclusion can yet be drawn.

Reporting: The process of preparing and presenting the information resulting from the analysis phase. Many factors affect reporting, including the following:

a. **Alternative Explanations:**When the information regarding an event is incomplete, it may not be possible to arrive at a definitive explanation of what happened. When an event has two or more plausible explanations, each should be given due consideration in the reporting process. Analysts should use a methodical approach to attempt to prove or disprove each possible explanation that is proposed.

b. **Audience Consideration:** Knowing the audience to which the data or information will be shown is important.

c. **Actionable Information:** Reporting also includes identifying actionable information gained from data that may allow an analyst to collect new sources of information

FORENSICS INVESTIGATION: Forensics are the scientific methods used to solve a crime. Forensic investigation is the gathering and analysis of all crime-related physical evidence in order to come to a conclusion about a suspect. Investigators will look at blood, fluid, or fingerprints, residue, hard drives, computers, or other technology to establish how a crime took place. This is a general definition, though, since there are a number of different types of forensics.

TYPES OF FORENSICS INVESTIGATION:

· Forensic Accounting / Auditing

· Computer or Cyber Forensics

· Crime Scene Forensics

· Forensic Archaeology

· Forensic Dentistry

· Forensic Entomology

· Forensic Graphology

· Forensic Pathology

· Forensic Psychology

· Forensic Science

· Forensic Toxicology

CHALLENGES IN COMPUTER FORENSICS:

Digital forensics has been defined as the use of scientifically derived and proven methods towards the identification, collection, preservation, validation, analysis, interpretation, and presentation of digital evidence derivative from digital sources to facilitate the reconstruction of events found to be criminal.But these digital forensics investigation methods face some major challenges at the time of practical implementation.

Digital forensic challenges are categorized into three major heads as per Fahdi, Clark, and Furnell are:

· Technical challenges

· Legal challenges

· Resource Challenges **TECHNICAL CHALLENGES** As technology develops crimes and criminals are also developed with it. Digital forensic experts use forensic tools for collecting shreds of evidence against criminals and criminals use such tools for hiding, altering or removing the traces of their crime, in digital forensic this process is called Anti- forensics technique which is considered as a major challenge in digital forensics world.

Other Technical challenges are:

· Operating in the cloud

· Time to archive data

· Skill gap

· Steganography **LEGAL CHALLENGES** The presentation of digital evidence is more difficult than its collection because there are many instances where the legal framework acquires a soft approach and does not recognize every aspect of cyber forensics, as in Jagdeo Singh V. The State and Ors case Hon'ble High Court of Delhi held that "while dealing with the admissibility of an intercepted telephone call in a CD and CDR which was without a certificate under Sec. 65B of the Indian Evidence Act, 1872 the court observed that the secondary electronic evidence without certificate u/s. 65B of Indian Evidence Act, 1872 is not admissible and cannot be looked into by the court for any purpose whatsoever." This happens in most of the cases as the cyber police lack the necessary qualification and ability to identify a possible source of evidence and prove it. Besides, most of the time electronic evidence is challenged in the court due to its integrity. In the absence of proper guidelines and the nonexistence of proper explanation of the collection, and acquisition of electronic evidence gets dismissed in itself.

Other Legal Challenges :

· Privacy Issues

· Admissibility in Courts

· Preservation of electronic evidence

· Power for gathering digital evidence

· Analyzing a running computer Resource Challenges As the rate of crime increases the number of data increases and the burden to analyze such huge data is also increasing on a digital forensic expert because digital evidence is more sensitive as compared to physical evidence it can easily disappear. For making the investigation process fast and useful forensic experts use various tools to check the authenticity of the data but dealing with these tools is also a challenge in itself.

Types of Resource Challenges are:

· Change in technology Due to rapid change in technology like operating systems, application software and hardware, reading of digital evidence becoming more difficult because new version software's are not supported to an older version and the software developing companies did provide any backward compatible's which also affects legally.

· Volume and replication The confidentiality, availability, and integrity of electronic documents are easily get manipulated. The combination of wide-area networks and the internet form a big network that allows flowing data beyond the physical boundaries. Such easiness of communication and availability of electronic document increases the volume of data which also create difficulty in the identification of original and relevant data

CYBERCRIMES: MOBILE AND WIRELESS INTRODUCTION.

Why should mobile devices be protected? Every day, mobile devices are lost, stolen, and infected. Mobile devices can store important business and personal information, and are often be used to access University systems, email, banking Proliferation of mobile and wireless devices:

a) people hunched over their smartphones or tablets in cafes, airports, supermarkets and even at bus stops, seemingly oblivious to anything or anyone around them.

b) They play games, download email, go shopping or check their bank balances on the go. They might even access corporate networks and pull up a document or two on their mobile gadgets Today, incredible advances are being made for mobile devices. The trend is for smaller devices and more processing power. A few years ago, the choice was between a wireless phone and a simple PDA.

Now the buyers have a choice between high-end PDAs with integrated wireless modems and small phones with wireless Web-browsing capabilities. A long list of options is available to the mobile users. A simple hand-held mobile device provides enough computing power to run small applications, play games and music, and make voice calls. A key driver for the growth of mobile technology is the rapid growth of business solutions into hand-held devices.

Mobile computing is "taking a computer and all necessary files and software out into the field." Many types of mobile computers have been introduced since 1990s.

They are as follows:

1. Portable computer: It is a general-purpose computer that can be easily moved from one place to another, but cannot be used while in transit, usually because it requires some "setting-up" and an AC power source.

2. Tablet PC: It lacks a keyboard, is shaped like a slate or a paper notebook and has features of a touchscreen with a stylus and handwriting recognition software. Tablets may not be best suited for applications requiring a physical keyboard for typing, but are otherwise capable of carrying out most tasks that an ordinary laptop would be able to perform.

3. Internet tablet: It is the Internet appliance in tablet form. Unlike a Tablet PC, the Internet tablet does not have much computing power and its applications suite is limited. Also it cannot replace a general-purpose computer. The Internet tablets typically feature an MP3 and video player, a Web browser, a chat application and a picture viewer.

4. Personal digital assistant (PDA): It is a small, usually pocket-sized, computer with limited functionality. It is intended to supplement and synchronize with a desktop computer, giving access to contacts, address book, notes, E-Mail and other features.

5. Ultramobile (PC): It is a full-featured, PDA-sized computer running a general-purpose operating system (OS).

6. Smartphone: It is a PDA with an integrated cell phone functionality. Current Smartphones have a wide range of features and installable applications.

7. Carputer: It is a computing device installed in an automobile. It operates as a wireless computer, sound system, global positioning system (GPS) and DVD player. It also contains word processing software and is Bluetooth compatible.

8. Fly Fusion Pentop computer: It is a computing device with the size and shape of a pen. It functions as a writing utensil, MP3 player, language translator, digital storage device and calculator.

Trends in Mobility: Mobile computing is moving into a new era, third generation (3G), which promises greater variety in applications and have highly improved usability as well as speedier networking. "iPhone" from Apple and Google-led "Android" phones are the best examples of this trend and there are plenty of other developments that point in this direction. This smart mobile technology is rapidly gaining popularity and the attackers (hackers and crackers) are among its biggest fans. It is worth noting the trends in mobile computing; this will help readers to readers to realize the seriousness of cybersecurity issues in the mobile computing domain. Figure below shows the different types of mobility and their implications.

The new technology 3G networks are not entirely built with IP data security. Moreover, IP data world when compared to voice-centric security threats is new to mobile operators. There are numerous attacks that can be committed against mobile networks and they can originate from two primary vectors. One is from outside the mobile network - that is, public Internet, private networks and other operator's networks - and the other is within the mobile networksthat is, devices such as data-capable handsets and Smartphones, notebook computers or even desktop computers connected to the 3G network.

Popular types of attacks against 3G mobile networks are as follows:

1. Malwares, viruses and worms: Although many users are still in the transient process of switching from 2G,2.5G2G,2.5G to 3G,3G, it is a growing need to educate the community people and provide awareness of such threats that exist while using mobile devices. Here are few examples of malware(s) specific to mobile devices:

· Skull Trojan: I targets Series 60 phones equipped with the Symbian mobile OS.

· Cabir Worm: It is the first dedicated mobile-phone worm infects phones running on Symbian OS and scans other mobile devices to send a copy of itself to the first vulnerable phone it finds through Bluetooth Wireless technology. The worst thing about this worm is that the source code for the Cabir-H and Cabir-I viruses is available online.

· Mosquito Trojan: It affects the Series 60 Smartphones and is a cracked version of "Mosquitos" mobile phone game.

· Brador Trojan: It affects the Windows CE OS by creating a svchost. exe file in the Windows start-up folder which allows full control of the device. This executable file is conductive to traditional worm propagation vector such as E-Mail file attachments.

· Lasco Worm: It was released first in 2005 to target PDAs and mobile phones running the Symbian OS. Lasco is based on Cabir's source code and replicates over Bluetooth connection.

2. Denial-of-service (DoS): The main objective behind this attack is to make the system unavailable to the intended users. Virus attacks can be used to damage the system to make the system unavailable. Presently, one of the most common cyber security threats to wired Internet service providers (iSPs) is a distributed denial-of-service (DDos) attack .DDoS attacks are used to flood the target system with the data so that the response from the target system is either slowed or stopped.

3. Overbilling attack: Overbilling involves an attacker hijacking a subscriber's IP address and then using it (i.e., the connection) to initiate downloads that are not "Free downloads" or simply use it for his/her own purposes. In either case, the legitimate user is charged for the activity which the user did not conduct or authorize to conduct.

4. Spoofed policy development process (PDP): These of attacks exploit the vulnerabilities in the GTP [General Packet Radio Service (GPRS) Tunneling Protocol].

5. Signaling-level attacks: The Session Initiation Protocol (SIP) is a signaling protocol used in IP multimedia subsystem (IMS) networks to provide Voice Over Internet Protocol (VoIP) services. There are several vulnerabilities with SIP-based VolP systems.

Credit Card Frauds in Mobile and Wireless Computing Era: These are new trends in cybercrime that are coming up with mobile computing - mobile commerce

(M-Commerce) and mobile banking (M-Banking). Credit card frauds are now becoming commonplace given the ever-increasing power and the ever-reducing prices of the mobile hand-held devices, factors that result in easy availability of these gadgets to almost anyone. Today belongs to "mobile compüting," that is, anywhere anytime computing. The developments in wireless technology have fuelled this new mode of working for white collar workers. This is true for credit card processing too; wireless credit card processing is a relatively new service that will allow a person to process credit cards electronically, virtually anywhere. Wireless credit card processing is a very desirable system, because it allows businesses to process transactions from mobile locations quickly, efficiently and professionally. It is most often used by businesses that operate mainly in a mobile environment

Security Challenges Posed by Mobile Devices:

Mobility brings two main challenges to cybersecurity: first, on the hand-held devices, information is being taken outside the physically controlled environment and second remote access back to the protected environment is being granted. Perceptions of the organizations to these cybersecurity challenges are important in devising appropriate security operating procedure. When people are asked about important in managing a diverse range of mobile devices, they seem to be thinking of the ones shown in below figure. As the number of mobile device users increases, two challenges are presented: one at the device level called "micro challenges" and another at the organizational level called "macrochallenges." Some well-known technical challenges in mobile security are: managing the registry settings and configurations, authentication service security, cryptography security,

Lightweight Directory Access Protocol (LDAP) security, remote access server (RAS) security, media player control security, networking application program interface (API), security etc.

Attacks on Mobile-Cell Phones:

· Mobile Phone Theft: Mobile phones have become an integral part of everbody's life and the mobile phone has transformed from being a luxury to a bare necessity. Increase in the purchasing power and availability of numerous low cost handsets have also lead to an increase in mobile phone users. Theft of mobile phones has risen dramatically over the past few years. Since huge section of working population in India use public transport, major locations where theft occurs are bus stops, railway stations and traffic signals.

The following factors contribute for outbreaks on mobile devices:

1. Enough target terminals: The first Palm OS virus was seen after the number of Palm OS devices reached 15 million. The first instance of a mobile virus was observed during June 2004 when it was discovered that an organization "Ojam" had engineered an antipiracy Trojan virus in older versions of their mobile phone game known as Mosquito. This virus sent SMS text messages to the organization without the users' knowledge.

2. Enough functionality: Mobile devices are increasingly being equipped with office functionality and already carry critical data and applications, which are often protected insufficiently or not at all. The expanded functionality also increases the probability of malware.

3. Enough connectivity: Smartphones offer multiple communication options, such as SMS, MMS, synchronization, Bluetooth, infrared (IR) and WLAN

connections. Therefore, unfortunately, the increased amount of freedom also offers more choices for virus writers.

- Mobile - Viruses
- Concept of Mishing
- Concept of Vishing
- Concept of Smishing
- Hacking – Bluetooth

Operating Guidelines for Implementing Mobile Device Security Policies In situations such as those described above, the ideal solution would be to prohibit all confidential data from being stored on mobile devices, but this may not always be practical. Organizations can, however, reduce the risk that confidential information will be accessed from lost or stolen mobile devices through the following steps:

1. Determine whether the employees in the organization need to use mobile computing devices at all, based on their risks and benefits within the organization, industry and regulatory environment.

2. Implement additional security technologies, as appropriate to fit both the organization and the types of devices used. Most (and perhaps all) mobile computing devices will need to have their native security augmented with such tools as strong encryption, device passwords and physical locks. Biometrics techniques can be used for authentication and encryption and have great potential to eliminate the challenges associated with passwords.

3. Standardize the mobile computing devices and the associated security tools being used with them. As a matter of fundamental principle, security deteriorates quickly as the tools and devices used become increasingly disparate.

4. Develop a specific framework for using mobile computing devices, including guidelines for data syncing, the use of firewalls and anti-malware software and the types of information that can be stored on them.

5. Centralize management of your mobile computing devices. Maintain an inventory so that you know who is using what kinds of devices.,

6. Establish patching procedures for software on mobile devices. This can often be simplified by integrating patching with syncing or patch management with the centralized

7. Provide education and awareness training to personnel using mobile devices. People cannot be expected to appropriately secure their information if they have not been told how.

Organizational Policies for the Use of Mobile Hand-Held Devices :

There are many ways to handle the matter of creating policy for mobile devices. One way is creating distinct mobile computing policy. Another way is including such devices existing policy. There are also approaches in between where mobile devices fall under both existing policies and a new one.In the hybrid approach, a new policy is created to address the specific needs of the mobile devices but more general usage issues fall under general IT policies. As a part of this approach, the "acceptable use" policy for other technologies is extended to the mobile devices. Companies new to mobile devices may adopt an umbrella mobile policy but they find over time the the they will need to modify their policies to match the challenges posed by different kinds of mobile hand-held devices. For example, wireless devices pose different challenges than non-wireless Also, employees who use mobile devices more than 20%% of the time will have different requirements than less-frequent users. It may happen that over time, companies may need to create separate policies for the mobile devices on the basis of whether they connect wirelessly and with distinctions for devices that connect to WANs and LANs .

Concept of Laptops: As the price of computing technology is steadily decreasing, usage of devices such as the laptops is becoming more common. Although laptops, like other mobile devices, enhance the business functions owing to their mobile access to information anytime and anywhere, they also pose a large threat as they are portable Wireless capability in these devices has also raised cyber security concerns owing to the information being transmitted over other, which makes it hard to detect. The thefts of laptops have always been a major issue, according to the cybersecurity industry and insurance company statistics. Cybercriminals are targeting laptops that are expensive, to enable them to fetch a quick profit in the black market. Very few laptop. thieves. are actually interested in the information that is contained in the laptop. Most laptops contain personal and corporate information that could be sensitive.. Physical Security Countermeasures Organizations are heavily dependent upon a mobile workforce with access to information, no matter where they travel. However, this mobility is putting organizations at risk of having a data breach if a laptop containing sensitive information is lost or stolen. Hence, physical security countermeasures are becoming very vital to protect the information on the employees laptops and to reduce the likelihood that employees will lose laptops.

1. Cables and hardwired locks: The most cost-efficient and ideal solution to safeguard any mobile device is securing with cables and locks, specially designed for laptops. Kensington cables are one of the most popular brands in laptop security cable. These cables are made of aircraft-grade steel and Kevlar brand fiber, thus making these cables 40%% stronger than any other conventional security cables. One end of the security cable is fit into the universal security slot of the laptop and the other end is locked around any fixed furniture or item, thus making a loop. These cables come with a variety of options such as number locks, key locks and alarms.

2. Laptop safes: Safes made of polycarbonate - the same material that is used in bulletproof windows, police riot shields and bank security screens-can be used to carry and safeguard the laptops. The advantage of safes over security cables is that they protect the whole laptop and its devices such as CD-ROM bays, PCMCIA cards and HDD bays which can be easily removed in the case of laptops protected by security cables.

3. Motion sensors and alarms: Even though alarms and motion sensors are annoying owing to their false alarms and loud sound level, these devices are very efficient in securing laptops. Once these devices are activated, they can be used to track missing laptops in crowded places. Also owing to their loud nature, they help in deterring thieves. Modern systems for laptops are designed wherein the alarm device attached to the laptop transmits radio signals to a certain range around the laptop. **4. Warning labels and stamps:** Warning labels containing tracking information and identification

details can be fixed onto the laptop to deter aspiring thieves. These labels cannot be removed easily and are a low-cost solution to a laptop theft. These labels have an identification number that is stored in a universal database for verification, which, in turn makes the resale of stolen laptops a difficult process. Such labels are highly recommended for the laptops issued to top executives and/ or key employees of the organizations.

5. Other measures for protecting laptops are as follows:

· Engraving the laptop with personal details

· Keeping the laptop close to oneself wherever possible

· Carrying the laptop in a different and unobvious bag making it unobvious to potential thieves

· Creating the awareness among the employees to understand the responsibility of carrying a laptop and also about the sensitivity of the information contained in the laptop

· Making a copy of the purchase receipt, laptop serial number and the description of the laptop

· Installing encryption software to protect information stored on the laptop

· Using personal firewall software to block unwanted access and intrusion

· Updating the antivirus software regularly

· Tight office security using security guards and securing the laptop by locking it down in lockers when not in use

· Never leaving the laptop unattended in public places such as the car, parking lot, conventions, conferences and the airport until it is fitted with an anti theft device;

· Disabling IR ports and wireless cards and removing PCMCIA cards when not in use. Information systems security also contains logical access controls. This is because, information, be it corporate or private, needs high security as it is the most important asset of an organization or an individual.

A few logical or access controls are as follows:

1. Protecting from malicious programs/attackers/social engineering.

2. Avoiding weak passwords/ access.

3. Monitoring application security and scanning for vulnerabilities.

4. Ensuring that unencrypted data/unprotected file systems do not pose threats.

5. Proper handing of removable drives/storage mediums /unnecessary ports.

6. Password protection through appropriate passwords rules and use of strong passwords.

7. Locking down unwanted ports/devices. 8. Regularly installing security patches and updates.

9. Installing antivirus software/firewalls / intrusion detection system (IDSs).

10. Encrypting critical file system

9 798886 673241

Printed by Libri Plureos GmbH in Hamburg, Germany